Knight Time Tea Travels

AUTHºR

KIRA KNIGHT-MCKAY

authorHOUSE®

AuthorHouse™
1663 Liberty Drive
Bloomington, IN 47403
www.authorhouse.com
Phone: 1-800-839-8640

First published by AuthorHouse 9/20/2010

ISBN: 978-1-4520-6671-4 (sc)

Library of Congress Control Number: 2010934652

Printed in the United States of America

This book is printed on acid-free paper.

For my dear hearts Khari & Khamora
Leave no rocks unturned, seek truth, embrace knowledge,
love hard, catch every star, and travel every moon,
and constantly smile.....smile, smile, smile..
Mommy loves you more, more, and more...xoxo

Dedication page

3 women inspire my every move:
Great grandmother Mrs. Mary D. Brown (RIP)
Grandmother Mrs. Marie L. Knight
Mommy Ms. Deborah M. Knight-Wills
From expressive talks, scholarly thoughts, fireworks in the
park or sharing some vanilla bean ice cream. The beam, glow, &
shine the way you held your heads up high
I honor you...

I dedicate to you Khari & Khamora; my every move is for
you. From you growing in my womb to your first steps and
everything you little minis ever want to do. Thoughts of you
both fill every space that was ever misplaced before I birthed
you; I see so much greatness & treasures in the both of you.
I more than LOVE you...

My dearest Tracey, this bliss is our top priority list. I have so
much to say, can thank you so many ways. Or how about it
husband we go on a hot date.
Adore you more, I see you, do you see me too...xoxo

Kira's cups of tea (contents)

Introduction

Year after year I found myself looking through my collection from the past 20 plus years of some 200 poems, songs, letters, short stories, notebooks full of my little to-do wish lists in a huge box staring at me everyday and every night from the corner of my room.

In November 2009 I finally convinced myself to try an item or two while working on my Master degree in Psychology. Taking on more than one task at a time would seem a bit much while raising a family but the urgency within me to fulfill at least one of my dreams would possibly lead to a domino affect of completed checks on my wish lists. The race started in my mind to start analyzing my list.

The feelings inside me went haywire, up and down, side to side with the judgment of giving away some of my closest journal inquiries wondering if items chosen would help myself or anyone at all. Another thought of strategizing what to compile, how to convey and where to get the extra money to do so kept me awake but in high spirits each and every night. I imagined and dreamed that one of these achievements can help shape or reshape myself and others that may have similar topics floating around in their lives.

I searched over my collections combined with long nights filled with drinking all sorts of tea varieties to stay awake, soothe, or cover hurt feelings. The thoughts I wrote as a young teenager mainly focused on the male figure discouragement, as they were not always positive and blissful. Most of the stories still had happy endings knowing one day a love poem of many multitudes would appear from my belief because of changes in my real life. As a young woman I would hold in my annoyed feelings so I could always portray to be happy and uncomplicated so others around me wouldn't feel the pain or run away from me. Wanting to know love, or just happy to think love could be kept me quiet verbally but screeching and screaming on the inside even when something was terribly wrong on the outside.

Raised by a single parent who had family assistance and resilience my mother always made sure I had outlets and entertainment. She kept me in after school programs, camps, and tried to celebrate every weekend like it was a holiday, all on a single parent, part-time working, and full-time college student budget. I never demanded material items, but was ecstatic to see what store packages she may have with her getting off the 49 bus everyday. She would bring home books, silver bangles, and clothes from the department discount centers from her long days in Newark, NJ's shopping area after taking classes at the University all day.

My grandmother always called me a trooper, a little uncomplicated girl with a lovely smile that was a pleasure to have around. I strove for independence at a young age. As a teen I put myself in the work world early. While in high school performing arts and media classes appealed to me so immediately after high school graduation I attended college for communications with hopes to work for media outlets in New York City. Working for various production companies and appearing in music videos and movies helped me with the experience when my mother wanted to move to northern California, although I wanted to stay on the east coast I moved myself to the Los Angles area and made the best I could of living in California on my own continuing in the show business field and keeping a full time job. Every obstacle, turning point, and reflection came to life in my journals that I kept hold of year after year.

When an offer to move back to the east coast arrived with the attachment of a music deal I jumped on it with hopes to be closer to home and to finish my college goals in between the contracted agreement. At college I began to open up in writing courses and poetry sessions. While my attention of love for tea & poetry together kicked in I soon was nicknamed The Tea Lady. After graduating with my AA degree in a music business management I left New York to move to Florida where my Grandparents and other close family members relocated to for the warmer weather. I immediately worked for various media companies and matriculated at a local University to obtain my BA degree in business management. Still keeping journals and adding to stories and thoughts of each new endeavor brought to my life.

Later I married a remarkable business man/DJ/radio personality and our union formed two magnificent children. Each step drew me closer and closer to writing short stories, poems and songs. Working on my Masters degree in Psychology opened my reflections again to dig deep in my soul to unload thoughts that are still issues today with optimism to convey, release, help and have others relate. With hopes people can see through their issues

get them checked early on with therapy and simple self-love.

I am hoping to unlock other ways to put my love of tea, love of words, love of helping each other to portray a more encouraging outlook for our selves, relationships, and everyday glitches to a forefront while keeping them all connected with my cup's of tea. ☺

I want to thank everyone for the support, love and bright blessings. I am happy to finally invite you to read with me and drink my cups of tea...

Knight Time Tea Travels...have a sip with me...

CHAPTER 1

Green Teas

hints of get-up-and-go
antioxidants has immense powers
organize the soul
fight off the control

Kira's cup of tea

Kira's about to share her soul
Hoping it will help mend
The past, future, & present within

Here's a saucer with a matching cup
Tired of calling my own bluff
Some issues were ruff and some not enough

Lot's of flavor's to acquire
Sit with me, put on the fire
Have a sip with me, or 3
I have lots of varieties

now tell me

How do you like your TEA?
Flaming hot or icy cold...

espresso crimes

I feel for you and your sick ways
adore you too, must be insane
Why is wanting u such a craze

Why is it, what's bad, feels so right?
In the middle of the moonlight
Writing you this rhyme

So I did decide to leave you tonight
But will I forever live a lie

Will I search for another
With the same irresistible eyes
Sipping espresso @ 3:09

Maybe it is a crime to depart your side
Knowing we still have a void
Everyone will forever know

Feeling like I'm just another toy
The souls just won't collide
Really should say goodbye

Why do I have to wait so long
For you to believe our love song

Really is my crime
Just to pass the time
Sipping espresso @ 3:09
Time to say goodbye...

mud survives

mud is murky
said to be morally impure
grimy to the unqualified eye
but what is it really??

Replenishing to the existence
A life that desires nourishment, a will to survive
Optimism can float
even thru the murky mud
when others would rather die

MUD SURVIVES

cloudy to some, but not to those with the qualified eyes...

DEAD PRESIDENTS

Money the root of the filth
Evil that it holds, greed that it molds
Has young girls looking incredibly old
Lil boys patrolling the corner like trolls
Waiting for the fiends to pay the toll
Hoping 5-0 won't pop the hoe stroll
All this for the hope of a stack of them dead presidents

Holes in the hearts of the pushers,
Watching the blood seep from the crack heads souls
All this for the power of them dead presidents

African gems, blood diamonds and gold's turn to powder
Muddy water fills the tubs (what cowards)
Hungry for a meal but more hungry for a 5-dollar holler high of
dust,
Bags of what they can smoke, shoot up, or toke
These sacks feed to the mental distortion, extortion of the spirit
For the lust of dead presidents

Pain is felt over and over again, new highs, new victims
Taxes used to keep it going taxes used to keep all employed
Hearts singing for the empty, grieving prayers for the diluted
blood
positive foundations never taught
Love lost, evil brought for the lust & thrills just to say who's rich
and who kills
A curse foreseen for the glitz & gleam
For a nation that still fiends for the love of them........Dead
Presidents....

1 and 2

Thoughts of my past
Some tranquil, some horrid
Plenty of flashbacks
Well.....
Thought about 1 or 2
That would gloom a yellow paisley room

Decided to give myself a memoir class......with class
Then burn the thoughts to ash

Spell it all out
Pass it out to the girls, boys, all so dear
Always telling them of valid facts in depth without fear
Never wanna neglect
Always pays respect
Gotta protect the parties that may have left

Won't pursue
Or try to sue
But there may have been 1 or 2
That gained me a distraught mood
Sure they may laugh
But I'll chuckle too
I know
They're still some lame dudes
Rude, shallow, &STILL looking for that obsession
to make there lives go
WOOHOO!!!

Boohoo to the 1 that raped my first heart
And him 2 who tried with a dagger and a broom
Dogs barked, doctors marked
Just a few things that could've been my doom

Could have used real names to convey defeat
My conquer never had to be too noise-say
Children pay attention
All that glitters is usually fools gold

Learn self respect, self protection
finicky you need to be
No it is not conceit
You may be called a geek, nerd, or a bore
Better than allowing them to score
Keeping tally of a how many they can steal, dishonor and kill
But children you may never heal

Block and shield

Don't get involved with those like 1 & 2,
Just searching for that painful raw feel...

This Time Has to Heal......

CHAPTER 2

<u>Mint & Ginger Teas</u>

Nature's wonder drugs
I confess
Fighting the stress
Pungent taste cures this disturbed
stomach
Helping me fight through this mess
Be blessed

The Absentees

so lonely
would you hold me?
where is mommy?
working late to pay the bills,
at the university acquiring her degree hoping for a better way
so lonely
but where is daddy
unknown, absent, and never checked in
shouldn't he be here, helping mommy
nope, guess he doesn't wanna be
so who is he? could I look like him, act like him too?
WHO KNEW!!!!!

I know she searched for you

Why don't you want us
She is beautiful, clean and careful
Drinks tea every night and day
Cooks healthy meals
With tofu, never eats steaks
Has a garden with cucumbers, tomatoes, kale and collards
Plants flowers just to help the bees pollinate, we love to sit &
watch for hours

Nurses me when I'm under the weather,
Holds me when the boys make me shed tears,

Destroyed all my fears

Reads to me about history, music, poetry and math year after
year
Dances with me in the rain put me in my first 4th of July
parade
Taught me how to roller-skate and bake a delicious chocolate
cake

The pretty lady even smiled when we would have to wait in line,
Picking up the absolutely "nutritious" government cheese,
Or hoping to get approved for aid like food stamps, milk,
health care,
school lunch tickets, and bus passes too
oh please don't stare
you know this is true, you have to care

Please!!! dear Lord help us PLEASE..... I could hear her cry
at night.....

Sneaking putting pennies together so I would never be aware
That my birthday parties were pulled together by the last
strands of her long graying hair
Even sent me off to camp with care packages filled of heart
felt devotion and flair

maybe you do not care,
does it even matter
one day you will recognize
or maybe an absentee could never ever understand
what is care
all we really needed you to do was just to hold our hands....

VODKA within HIM

"Hey roller"
You'll never make it
You're too skinny, kinda funny looking too
You remind me of my sister
I HATE YOU

You'll never make it
Love will never find you
Listen to me when I yell at you
A novice never wins
I HATE YOU

Don't you know where I've been?
Went to the Philippines, had dinners with the Japanese,
Jumped 50,000 feet from fighter jets
You'll never do that I bet

If you dash past I may trip or even choke your ass
"Watch it roller"
no body ever loved me,
no one will ever love you
you're just a filthy yellow nigga
just like me
and I hate you...

the reply to him:

well I just wanna say thank you
I've never used your words of hate,
To relate

Remember you are the one who took the training wheels off
my purple hand-me-down bike
You made sure I learned before twilight
Your face was proud as can be
Even taught me to swim before I was three

As you can see I always loved you, knew it wasn't you
Just the disease of alcohol stealing your soul
blending you all shades of blue
That's the part evil loves to control
Evil loves to grasp once happy souls

"BEHOLD"

Even as a little girl I knew
You didn't want me to turn out like you
But I will always love you no matter what and I thank you...

The Monster left the room

18 years after the act
his dark skin turned extra pale
ashamed & shocked to be exact
to see the young woman he once failed

remembered that cold wet winter night
how he dragged her by her hair
she screamed call 911 in the restaurant
but not a soul even cared
threw her in the truck
he hydroplaned all the way there
she tried to take a leap
but he held grasp of her Rapunzel like hair
remembered how she begged
"door man please help me if you care"
monster just gave the door man
a cash tip with his slithery cold hand
still grasping her hair firmly with the right
then tossed her down his stairs

entered the room of despair
where she did nothing but try to get away from there
she cried and cried
how did she end up in a monster's lair

his caged dogs barked while he ripped off all her clothes
pulled off her boots
then continually bashed her diamond pierced nose

his bare hands

choked her till she couldn't breath for air
used a collection of walking sticks
to belt & change her beautiful tanned skin
to shades of black, green, blue and a slight hue of brown too

dangled her out the window
warned her if she told
even if he went to prison
she would be tortured till she's old

she finally fainted
of thoughts she should just let it all go

she woke an hour later confused to see
the monster entering in and out inside her hole
he was crying and praying
over her multi colored shaded thin body
Why do these monsters prevail?

she hoped someone would find her
prayed just send her home
AT LAST

a whole day or two later he finally let her go

the monster left the room
murdered her virginity
used torture for his control
how do these monsters exist
the sick coldhearted souls

today the heathen monster looks withered and frail
shooting heroin feeding the monstrous desires that all failed

He must have had a behavioral issue or 2 way back in 1982

Saw him from across the room

Now on his last leg, toothless, and penniless
Felt a lil sorry for the fiend
But she snickered deep inside
Turned and walked the other way
To control her toothy smile
18 years ago that's the same sick monster that attempted
to steal her life, and beautiful smile...

3 days to your destruction

Day 1, now you're distressed, don't you regret
the curse is now reversed
splurge is what you used to do
with your condoms and that screw-a-chick crew
so now your feeling it, yes it's true
apologetic faces you elude in front of your troop
I guess you thought I'd die for you after this ploy
"Please"
And have my momma and aunties sent away for murdering you
"Never would do that"

Day 2, as you see, it's not cool to get pulled into scandals and
schemes
thought WE were a team
a dream still not fully conceived
men still mentally do not understand
I see
Even after witnessing the births of babies 1, 2 and 3,
almost had baby# 4
if it wasn't for all your whores
Oh how you swore
you would change your course
even showed plenty of remorse back in 1989, and 2004

Day 3, you swore I was too weak to step
how you were so happy to keep this Goddess barefoot and pregnant
how do you feel all the country knows
"you secretly woe"
you violated the terms of this kinship,
when you joined this top-secret world of so-called "friendships"...

excuses

all about the feeling
all about the heart
jumpstart the dead
the battery needs to be charged
Can't deny
thought you were the one
feeding off each other
but there is no truth
or needs, never planted the seeds
feelings are farce
souls ending up sparse
obviously a curse on you
and me
I usually get back luck after day 3
Excuses, excuses
But why do I get stuck with losers...

While u were out

Hey dear
While u were out
Ur briefcase made a ringing noise
A secret cell phone I guess
Trying to fill a void????
A she telephoned 4 u
strange voice over the phone
seemed to be my clone
she wouldn't stop phoning
4am, 4:15, and 4:30pm
WOW!!!
what a friend

guess what
she returned YOUR call
claims u call her a lot
even met u in our private parking lot
secret rendezvous
while I'm at the shop

WOW HUBBY, HOW FREAKING HOT!!

One day she thought
How u almost got caught
Kept stroking steady poking to hit the spot
Claims you pursue her a lot

THIS HAS GOT TO STOP!!

Recently she came to see u

During my shop hours
I kept quiet in the quest shower
Watched it all
What a bunch of cowards
U were all up in her flowers
Watched u drink her nectar
Then feed her garden, u wet her
Demon seeds u planted
Will NEVER be ours

WAIT AND SEE, U WILL BOTH GET YOURS!!

Left a message on the wall
Please call
her tulip will be stillborn
This May will bring a gloomy day
As it may
Yes I am awfully scorned
witnessed the ease you deceive
Not cool to play
GET GONE
Family torn
Because of u fertilizing your dirty little weeds...

gone

My eyes are open
I can finally see
Still bleeding though
From all the pain you infested within me,
Thanks to you and all your trickery
Stealing others love, raw and uncut like a disease
Do u not care how u personalize that gift?
You with your so-called souvenir that was never wanted or needed
inside of here

The blood is slowly stopping
Told myself death was not the option
Breathing is easy again,
My eyes are no longer diluted
Healing may not ever be, but leaving is a superior start to me
Following my heart,
feeling the beat was new today; cause the beat was only for you
Now it is free to beat and beat loudly just for me!!

Who would have known?
I could save my soul
I'm outta that zone, won't even search for your clone
Hope your happy, exploiting hearts, leaving your disease is your art,
I am just proud I learned to set myself free

I AM GONE!!!!

My eyes are open,
I can finally see
I actually feel sorry for those other 3......

CHAPTER 3

Red Roobios & Passionflower Teas

Promoting my good nights sleep,
Without caffeine
Pure & natural, no sugar needed
The herbs cool my nerves
Sweet taste beyond compare
Thirst quenching & easing my soul
I like to drink it bare

something you need?

Should I love the feeling or just the thought
I if let you make a move will I end up distressed
Opening the door could just start a game
A competition of you pursuing me till you got me,
What then??

If setting the tone from the start doesn't relay
If writing my policy on your forehead won't calculate
What then?

So, is this something you really need?
Is this just how you feed your self-esteem?
Will you play with my head?
While you have 3 or 4 others sleeping in your bed
I ask that you be honest, is that so hard,
I need to know your plan before and IF we ever do start

So tell me.....I am really someone you need?
Because a heart is heart.......let's part or proceed???...

Frankincense & Myrrh

a new phase
seeing through the haze
all the world knows now
oceans and mountains sing out loud
two souls now bound
from the heavens
through the clouds

the moon is always full a perfect sphere for me & you
galaxies unite
all glistens for you & I
Mars snoops and Venus listens too
2 unicorns soar high, mystical to the eyes
blessed and pure
just notice the cure

for miles and miles
centuries and years
galaxies and worlds
this love brings delight and cheer
too all the good Angels
and every Saint far and near...

iced tea, hot tea

You gave me too much iced tea
Left me feeling hyper, at times queasy
Uneasy and suppressed
Feeding off the broken heart you've possessed
can I let go of this misery and call this quits
Being on edge with a sugar rush is the fucking pits
can I set sail and leave your side

Wonder how it will feel to ride a new tide
Replace your vibe
Fly high past your mansions, mountains and sands
discover a new land

maybe if I try hot tea
this could be a plan

YES!!!

drinking it leaves me relaxed and calm
enlightens my stride
but how come
I can't forget about the wrecked heart I have inside
A sad comply to the delight hot tea brings

Keep hearing my murdered heart sing:

"add more honey & lemon"
"get the right taste, let's start a new beginning"
"let's mend this injury one sip at a time"
"we can't keep singing the same sad line"

"put that iced tea drinking to it's final end"
"Now don't let me tell this u this over and over again!!!!"

why, yes you are so right

Please pass the honey & lemon
Hot tea,
You're my new best friend
thanks a million for the new beginning....

love poem......

love could be here
a flicker of the bold brown eye
happy tears are near
a long sigh
a forever high
loves justice is finally here

yesterday it seemed so far
today thanking GOD
for the angel man sent by love
never knew this would be in the cards
inside cheers
love is so clear

love is like the spring's birth
this time will never be reversed
love is happy even when our pockets are broke
shining through storm clouds, this ain't no joke
moons seem to always be full
stars dazzling ever so bright

feeling the storm, the most wondrous blizzard
flickers of lightning
wind gusts cools, rains cleanse
the universe rules
the spell of love
controls and soothes....

Full Moons

Full moons always shine
Full moons always get me HIGH
My best time to unwind,

Pass the hot green tea with honey please,

sigh

Now I cry

Full moons make me realize how much
I miss you,
How much I treasured you
Full moons make me understand why I desired you.

Why every 29.53 days gives me that reflection
Of what it felt like to have known
the secret mystical man of the moon

Am I distraught? Should I keep this hush-hush?
still amazed with past images & thoughts

The last full moon ended with me remembering,
that intent look of your silvery almond shaped eyes...

Again I sighed...on to another to cry

Suppose I Will need a lifetime supply
Is the kettle still warm?
please pass more
green tea & honey
Amore, amore......

Nag Champa Stick

Light a match to my stick
Of my favorite incense
Relaxed in this meditative state of mind

Saw through the smoke
the man with those intense eyes
thoughts provoked my mind
the moonlight shines

He stepped into my sight
Oblivious to his name
His eyes are keeping me tame
passionate yet insane

Could it be a spiritual gaze?
Or the nag champa haze
Of why he never strayed

Lost all my game
He didn't come here to play
The man with those intense eyes
Cleansing my high

Love this smoke filled wind of change
Promise I will never stray
Thank you for this spiritual vibe

burn another nag champa stick
or some super hit incense
This time lets burn side by side...

Traveling through tropical tea

Earth moving
Moon's fullness
Shining lights
Starry nights

Flowers blooming
Merchants of love flying
From tree to tree
Singing tropical songs as early as 3:53

Loves in the air
Singing past our ears
Exotic fruit fill our souls
Blended vanilla's & coconut smells
Controls our hold
Mangoes, bananas and kiwis fill our bowl
Indulge

This feeling is the sanity
No vanity
Mansions, fancy cars, diamonds and such
Won't matter as much
What this brings
Is much like the rites of spring
love combined with a this ring...

dance

dancing alone in my mind
seems kinda wrong
but your always gone
time still doesn't combine
so I still imagine a slow wind
quiet and alone

I need us to dance
to some smooth jazz
r& b kings
dem knotty dreads
disco queens
or hip hop heads
a tone and a beat
dancing
used to be so easy

all we need
is a moment or 3
me & you
you & me
need to let loose and dance
don't miss our chance
don't let it slip by
no time to cry

don't need new shoes
clean the car
or hit a bar
my five-inch heels could do

barefoot would even be nice
you shouldn't have to think twice
to dance and live life

we can even dance in our yard
this shouldn't be so hard
grab my hand you take lead
a walk to the park
dance in the grass till dark

admire the stars
thank the Heavens, Venus and Mars
that we still want to dance
only with each other
and I don't mean with those whorish deterrents
like her, her, and him

just you and I
stare into each other's eyes
time to remember why
we used to enjoy each others dance...

CHAPTER 4

Chamomile Teas

my mutli herbal cure all
mild taste and trust
calming yet fortifying
repairing colds,
even cramping sickly holds

Multicultural

Cooked collard greens n cornbread on Friday
Cooking some fish fry with a dash of curry this Monday
Chewing on veggie kabobs, tabouli, and warm pita bread today
Red beans and rice I can never deny at any time
Add some sweet plantains if u please!!!
Fry bread and corn satisfies my spirit every time
Almond croissant for breakfast with steamy earl grey tea

"Indeed"

What are you cooked up to be?
Several family connections of nationalities
Flow through the blood within me
I am happy to be
All these varieties illustrate little Miss Kiwi.....

the number 1 & me

funny to know
same bloodline
close and aware
so why do they stare
dissecting every detail of the time
each and every occasion
making up issues in your mind
wanting us to fight
instead we protect
is the connection making you jealous
it is you that makes a big deal out of this

relations should be pleased
guarding one another
making the road paved with ease
not walking around with eyes of green
blowing off steam, your world displeased
when while you stop/at age 63?

she and I bond with simplicity
not my fault or number 1's
we obtained our degrees
danced at the sea
went to all the fairs
combed each other's hair
sorry u aren't aware

please
stray of childish schemes
be happy number one is the favorite

as I am her number 1
no regrets
why is it such a problem
we vibe
we ride
we dream
even hated the same peas
till we were age seventeen
number one is close to me as can be
why does this aggravate thee

went to all the shows
traveled across the globe
took care of her since she was 2, yet I was only 4
we never grew bored of our chores
long as we could sing while we dust
long as we had each other there
kept each other in line during trying times
made each laugh while eating garlic crabs
have each other's back, may even attack

yes we agree and at times disagree
few small issues of course, but stuck by each other through
each course

number 1 & me
we laugh now
over the problems others bring about
but kin is kin
so sorry you have doubt about your own clout
same seeds and still trying to compete
set yourself free
enjoy some tea with honey with she and me

You're always invited in
insecure horns get loose
tattle tailing begins
if you are grown why pretend
the same adolescent complaint over and over again
all because number 1 & me drink tea on repeat
enjoy brunches
turn Sundays into holidays
laughter and amaze
over the smallest of things

but u still sway and complain
I feel betrayed
tired of the head games
exhausted
conveyed, so I stayed away
stop portraying me to others in a bad way
then u get irate
number 1 takes up for me, as I do for she

easy to see
when I speak, too many competes
too many protests
putting up signs and slogans/wanna arrest?
making up crimes in your mind
green eyes seem to never cease
let it be
have some tea
live life with ease number 3...

for better or worse

Never noticed a difference
Of good hair or bad
Always cared less
If ones eyes were blue, brown or hashed

Shouldn't even matter what u have
credit or cash

What's the big deal with diverse colors of skin
Why should it make so many individuals mad
All hold the same color blood within
If u follow your tree we could all be some kin

Praying one day this will just be a story of the past
Dignity will surpass...

Prove or get approved from New York to Hollywood

Soon the inside secrets unfold
Can't pretend, can't withhold

Behold a few of my untold scrolls

When you begin to feel the vibe
You can't stop

Some items I witnessed were pretty nuts
Won't say any of your names, ya'll know who u are
how proud your family & friends truly are
but everyone knows a star is a star

issues that make the ordinary
4ever cold or sick in the guts
but everyone swears this town is a must

so was told once I had a nice butt
then it was too small, then not big enough

then to my clothes
dressed like a boy they said
told to spruce myself up with some shiny red f-me-pumps
instead

there was this case
had to prove my race
And explain all the freckles on my face
Why one day my hair was straight
And the next curled

Just accept me as I am
U people make me want to hurl

diamond ring in my nose, wasn't commercial enough

Damm...when is enough!! Enough??

another time back then
had to stop him from raping my friend
and who would have ever thought
he was that type of man
and he still plays pretend
still never got caught

one offered me a breast job
said a hand full was not what's up
for this industry role
told myself I won't lose my soul
or try to cover them up
and guess what
still happy with my 2 little perfect plums

AH HA Fool WHAT!!!!

another proposed he should knock me up
wanted a child with freckles & such
but couldn't be around for all the important stuff
a fat check wasn't really enough
to have my body spread its guts
for a sick rich nut

a few of you thought I would be distraught
if u really knew back then

what I always thought

mostly a pocket full of fools
with pockets full of dust
money hungry cartoons
everyone gets overly made up

walking through the mall
dressed like a whore
hopes of being the next big box office score
or maybe just the weekly one to bust a few nuts
how caught up

men and women demonstrate
a portrait of self hate
just to prove or get approved
from east to west
minds are such a mess
thanks to the images

it's time to get blessed...

the letter

I regret
recently your company informed me
of how you could not take the chance
of placing my picture in your calendar and magazine
because of my skin color
I was taught to understand
I am a person made up of a multitude of colors, features and
hues
representing a real potpourri
this discrimination served me is unique
in that it represents the worst imaginable
it emanates from the minds of my own sisters and brothers
as a race of people we had to overcome years of racism just to
exist
but in 1995??
Are we psychologically damaged
Racism is not the only problem
It is sad to see struggles left us all enemies to each other
Was anything learned from out heroes??
If a "light" skinned black cannot find room in their own race
And not white, where does a lighter version of you belong??
On another planet perhaps???
How ironic MY family displays all hues
From the lightest to the darkest
From eyes of grays to browns
Hair from straight, curly, wavy, and yes some a lil nappy
A collection of love and features
African Americans are not carbon copies
Some just take back, this is how our rainbow reacts
Blacks are just as guilty as the white race

Brainwashing still exists
Resentment displayed leaves me
disappointed
abandoned
distrustful
hurt
thank God I have no problem accepting my race
I was raised in a black environment
Therefore have a black conscience
As well as learning the other races combined within me
Before you state what you do not know about me
Look up your own family tree
See how far your roots go...

many states, cities, & towns

love by far
far from love
can't count the lovers lost
but plenty of love goes around
quick love they get free in every state, city and town
leaving empty love hoping for a solid ground
gigantic smiles ending with enormous frowns,
from entertaining their sexual prowl
9 months later
a new child is born
in every state, city and town
leaving an ample of lovers scorned
families torn
when the events come around...

NEW ORLEANS

What is rich?
Is it the deep fried art of the Native Americans?
Is rich the deep pounding joyous drum rhythms of the African
slaves
Could it be the jazz the winds sing?
The Zydeco beats keeps us movin our feet
Could it be the all the traditions intertwined, to make a great
potpourri combined

Running so deep from the Square to where the Gulf of
Mexico meets
Spiritual & mystical, like the Cajun seasonings your crawfish
pot greets
The French, The Spanish, the swing and sway of the Creole
soul
Or is it Treme' ....the oldest black neighborhood full of
character
behold
a massive significance of history
The French Quarter intimate and distinctive
passions for our attention,
"I just wanted to mention"

What is rich?
Rich is what all the flavors teach,
Rich is the spirit we keep
Rich is the deep rooted essence of all the foods, arts, style of
architecture taught
Where Kings and Queens still roam the streets
Fabulous Krewes that leave us in awe

Rich is what can't be accomplished through crime
Rich is what the greedy can never see even when they paid
their dimes
Rich goes beyond the money made and bills paid
Being rich is in the hearts & souls,
That runs through the veins of families full of gold
Rich is pure love
Rich is what New Orleans holds, way down deep in the city's
soul
"Let the good times roll"......

Ms."O"

Not the normal TV host
More than the normal superstar
genuine and direct
you know who u are

has mass amounts of intellect
conquered interviews with Presidents,
and locals from Chi-town to Mars

insight always awesome keeping us aware
some issues brightly cheerful
and some that just aren't fair

it's been so superb to see
a brown woman with integrity and curves
like the women in my family tree
full of history

showcased daily I think around 4, could be 3
as long as I can sip my tea
a safe to be
in front of my TV

champion for all
from the very vanillas to the darkest cherry chocolates
makes plenty of common sense
she's so chic & stylish
bet she is compassionate,
see how she treats her pets

showed us how to vent, then leaves it up to the stars

now I gotta go
time to catch up with my imaginary homegirl
Ms. O
a safe to be
as u can see
in front of my TV @ 3
with a cup red of tea...

musical dreams

simple to some
but not yet to me
a dream
to learn and play the
Fur Elise
Beethoven's beautiful music
Song so sweet
It's always on repeat

Oh if I could learn to play
the structural chord
In Purple Haze
Like when Hendrix soared
And kissed the sky
I would cry

And how smart I could be
To write songs like he
The great king of Reggae
A Mellow Mood I'd be
Keeps my mind smooth n sweet
Mr. Marley thank you indeed

To sing like she
The Angel of Peace
I could Move on up a lil Higher
Sing and rejoice like she
Mahalia's voice
Was the greatest gospel voice to me

51

To lead a band,
Write songs and wave my hands
Controlling great jazz or swing bands
Like the charismatic, the eloquent
Mr. Duke Ellington

To have the deepest heartfelt feel
potent presence
graceful in face
no matter the year
to have the sweetest taboo
Like No Ordinary Love
Sade keeps my ear
And controls my love fears

A group funky with thrill
From my hometown Plainfield
Made me grab a Flashlight
And dance in my room all night
The Parliament funk is so freakin' outta sight

On to the NEPTUNES
Production living through the veins
Funk rock band with hip-hop too
Produced for all types of clones
But I like it best when I can stage dive
The group called N.E.R.D.
Doper than you all deserve
design my on clothes
Selling to my friends and foes

To have the complex lyrical flow
Studied by one and all, grabbing the mic with no pause

Rakim Allah the great, make no mistake
My Melody says it all
Being righteous yet keeping my metaphors deep
Enthralled

Got way too much to say
about the Prince a musical king
How the heck did he learn
all those instruments as a teen
a musical genius I see
songs so deep, catch the vibes
listen to 1999

Well as you can see
Music helps me think
Grew up through a lot
While my mom taught me about most
Hearing music to me is like being able to breath
Music I toast
The host of my musical dreams...

CHAPTER 5

Black Teas

Essence runs so deep
Richest in taste
Keeping me wide awake
My lil heart tonic, sweet with
honey & cream
Virus warrior, immune rebel
Soul survivor
PROCEED

1929

why on earth was it labeled
a year so miserable & hateful
the great depression they say
WELL
call it what they may

but to me & all related to me
believe
1929 an Angel was born,
yet in human form
she's the guardian of us all
the baby doll of the royal Mrs. Mary D. Brown
and the noble Mr. Moses Brown Jr.
she deserves more than diamonds & roses
Give her the whole entire mall
tickets to the moon
Castles and mansions
A new home every June
But she just wants to love us

funny how she still only wants to show
just how she really cares
even though she was shown & seen some of the worst of
things
some beyond you're most horrid of dreams
YET
never compared or even shed a tear

in 1929 economic times
did prove a tough and a cruel era

but whatever, whatever
it never showed in her face
another Grandma would never take her place

her blood bleeds thru me
I carry it with grace
Strong and secure
righteous, imperial, and majestic
She is always the top of my quest list
Would never think to dismiss this

Just wanted to say
July 4, 1929 was a splendid day

I thank you for
Guidance, and the cure
Your heart and soul
Even your tone
Soothes me to the core

Your attitude, quality and character
Makes me smile really huge
When I think of you

Glad you're here to read my poem
I love you Ma, Marie
Queen of the family throne...

The Gown

1949 a wedding dress was purchased
for Marie
at Oppenheim Collins in New York City
by Aunts Cora Lee & Susie Wilhelmina
the gown's material was off-white satin rose brocade on top of
satin
Mandarin styled collar with matching buttons down the chest
Made this dress stylish & priceless
worn by the Marie L. Brown on her wedding day
to marry William V. Knight Sr. September 25, 1949

the gown was kept in a cedar chest
tucked away out of existence
seemed no one had a need
for this dress
such an exquisite, sophisticated, elegantly styled gown
would it ever be worn again

1988, 39 years later
her first granddaughter Kira
was on a hunt for a gown for her senior high prom
visits to various gown stores in New Jersey and New York
became a bore
every visit became a chore, too many crowds, and too much
frustration
and none of the gowns suited her taste

that next weekend female family members gathered in Marie's
kitchen
the topic of a prom gown search came up

Kira's Aunt Donna made a suggestion
"let's see if Kira can fit into your wedding gown"
Donna at that time was a beauty editor for Woman's World
Magazine
She had impeccable taste
Kira & Marie agreed

the gown, retrieved from the cedar chest
the dress was in remarkable shape and color
onto Kira's body for a fitting
fit was so perfect, the tailor couldn't believe
Marie wore this gown 39 years before
to cut the gown into a waltz length
was the only alteration Kira wanted or needed
Kira's suggestion for the bottom material to become a cape
Saved and made
the attire looked like storybook garb
matching heels with rose brocade seemed to pop up
after checking in just one store at the local mall

Marie was happy to see her gown & her first granddaughter
off to the prom that May in'88
Marie's heart filled with happiness to see
all the efforts become more than worthwhile
Kira and the gown with delicate & intricate features came
home that evening
With the honor of being crowned prom queen of the high
school ceremony

The gown was meant to be

September 25th, 1993,
Kira's mom Deborah married in Santa Cruz, Ca

Kira wore the gown again this time to attend her mother's
wedding
44 years after the first wearing by Marie in September 25th,
1949

The gown preserved by Kira in May 2008
with hopes her daughter Khamora
would one day wear the gown
the gown with occurrence, elegance, so chic with traveling
feet...

cousins, sisters, friends

could of known u from way back then
my feelings were never pretend
some of you are brand new
I care for all you ladies to the end
Just wanted all my girls to know
You are all like
silver & gold
Gucci & Coach
D&G & Jimmy Choo
I just wanted to amuse
All my hot gal crew
1 or 2 of u even taught me how to hot curl
fixed each other's ponytails
cheerleading in the park
may even have jumped double-dutch till dark
took care of each other when we were broke
helped each other get grown
doubled dated and such
concern when the lovers scorned
had herbal tea to help the hearts mend
brunches or lunches
concerts, events, malls, a few sweet 16 balls
dine on red wines
memories new and old
good moods or bad
I will forever be glad
We shared fabulous sisterhoods
Give courage to one another
when we need to man up and dance
whatever the case
I love each grace
your faces hold in my hearts place...

pursued her from the very start
discarded all others to follow his heart
couldn't settle on a factor
on how to harass her

"let him know she wouldn't be so discounted
been there done that years before this meet, dumped those creeps
be sincere not just complimentary she said,
need to make sure he was not a disguised gentlemen
gonna be a bit pickier now, can't play pretend
already had 1 or 2 engagements from way back when"

his deep thoughts on how on earth to get at her
talks for hours
walks in summer rain showers
lunch meetings that would only last half an hour
invite her to a show, clutch hands in the mall and gloat
hoping after each meeting she would still take his calls
believing in her made him climb the walls

"I wonder if she'd swoon for a dozen rosy flowers
Some candy and wine, I hope she will smile for hours
Or a diamond ring,
Yes, this would be the honest thing"

paused for a thought
she is really a great catch
praying he finally met his match
not worried about a change of intellect

his mind was now blissful & exact

alarmed his mom,
boasted to his dad
of the new daughter in law they would soon include in the clan

told all the fellas
but they warned him

"you don't wanna go there
more fish we need to fry
more rewards to spot and plot,
take your time, drink something stronger than that wine
don't play yourself on a freckle-faced dime
in due time we will all have a life full of monogamy and years of
strife
come on man let go, stop wasting your time"

paused for a second, because he is no coward,
alerted all the fellas loud and clear

"come next season your all invited to an marvelous affair
And yall all better be there
Oh and don't forget to shower, shave and cut your hair"
See you there....
And oh yeah, thanks for all your concern & care...

My Moon, My Star

This was meant to be
Never knew it would come true
They give me that high
taller than
Those designer shoes,
Expensive cars,
And every leather bag I may never use

My moon, my star
Qualities are exquisite
terms may never clarify
this fabulous soar
loving you will never be a bore
you both may never realize
how much I truly adore

your sweet smiles
tender eyes
hugs in every size
picnics in the parks
projects from art
fill up my room
this is mommy's love
you both make me drool

sometimes when u sleep
praying you're blessed, God please keep
I start to weep
I gently kiss your hands, nose and feet
I love this hold

The moon and stars above me know
How much u mini's actually mean to me

Watching my roses grow
I hope you both really know
You own my heart, and every ounce of my soul...

DARE

Care?
What will people say
Who cares, do you
Dream that impossible dream
Dare yourself, just be

Does it matter who says what,
Strut your stuff
Tuck in that butt
Glide your on way
Imagine and sow
Plant those seeds
Water, nurture, and sing
They will grow
See the splendor of your very own glow
A rose, a petal or just a narrow stem

"How impossible they always said
Be simple, please don't shine
Don't bump your head
Put all your dreams to bed"

Forget what the haters said!!!!

I dare you
Dare you to cultivate
Dare you to stare yourself in the looking glass

GLARE

You can only be you
No stars
No stripes
No flashing lights
Just you
Who can be better than that???

Never compare
Just dare
I dare you...

CHAPTER 6

Almond Tea

Sweet delicacy
No need for a pastry
A dab of honey or raw sugar
The almond flavor
Cures the sweet tooth
Enjoy it sizzling hot
Too sweet for some
But not for me

Beaches

long for the days
can't wait for the suns haze
playing footsies in the sand
doesn't matter which land
the air cleans my sores
the salt water refreshes my souls
natural and perfect
picnics
dates
weddings
child's castles
baptisms
fishing
walking for miles
collecting the treasures
hope to find a starfish
send it back and make a perfect wish
soak my feet
write down all my dreams
in the sand
let the ocean goddess hear my prayers
each shell I take home gives me hope
knowing happiness is near
no fear
sea air hugs my body
the sand in my hair
the sun kissing very inch of my skin
the salty water cures the giant bruises again
thank you
can't wait to enjoy

natures perfect hospital food
feeling so fresh
polished and vibrant
thank u God for sharing
thank you for making me new
the beaches repair
smell the air
unwind and conceive
beaches purify
make time
pull off your shoes and try...

kissing me

she wakes
love is always near
a stare, a kiss, a hug, before she even combs her hair
not even one
but two
a kiss from her and he
how blessed
how honored
how fortunate
how approved
these 2 little kisses fill her room
before she even stands on her feet
love is effortless
love is with ease
love is gazing at he and she
love is more than acceptance from the streets
love is what the 2 sweet voices give to she
mean more than the car keys
more than the shoes, purses, and flair
look at the simplicity of the kisses
she can breathe/knowing a kiss is near and precious
The love of the two
fills any empty space
even erased the displaced
before they came to be
kiss of love
a kiss
a kiss
a mommy's perfect wish
love is more than the parade

before they arrived
love is what her kisses
convey
more than words can really say
how her hearts sinks
how her eyes tear
when they kiss their mommy year after year

I must confess
I give my all to you
My two little dears...

home or house

pick what you need
home or house
only one breathes devotion
only one keep care
only one shelters
only one is warm
only one has the smell of love in the air
the home or the house can be bare or filled
home or the house which do u feel is real
one holds & keeps your dreams
one is only for cheap thrills and fiends
one is strong and loaded with real respect and care
one is just because weakness is put in your ear from fear
home or the house
which do you need
or
which do you think u want
think hard
believe
do you get these two mixed up
home or house
do you have a thought
what makes sense in the end
buckle down
time is running out my friend...

white candle

feeling intense
needing light
wanting clarity

vanilla smells entice
almonds, or coladas are even nice

soothes the atmosphere
helps to the prelude
let go of a bad mood
white candle
absorb and let it go
helps tie in the prayers of this positive protection plan
white candle may even wane
that's okay I prayed
always in God's hands
trusting the higher plane
believing is transmitted
believing is brought to glow
eyes closed
or
eyes bright
God's love unites
In my candle light
Blessings released
White candle helping the insight
Relaxed feeling alright
Sipping on herbal almond white
Looking through the candle light
God's love is always clear

God's love unites
diminishes fears
God's love shows the reason for tears
Makes the smiles more sincere
White candle always shining bright
Those that are confused may never see
Not understanding but hear me
Through the white flame God gave to thee
Priceless/ love is always revealed
Here is one for you from me
White candle, consider and see
God will shine through darkness and brightness
God's presence is meant to always be
Believe and breathe, blessed be...

Simba Sue

Call it what u may
She always made my day
By my side from state to state
Never cried or ran away
Simple and pure
Stayed for 12 years or more
Some could never relate
But my feelings were great
Her white paws touched my hands
That birthday I grabbed her out of my book bag
Fell in love, she was tiny as a cup
1994 she was born sick and covered in muck
Grew healthy full of love and trust
She was the bee's knees,
TO ME!!!!!!
Made sure she got all my hugs
She even accepted my dates
But stayed away from the fakes
That's how I knew those dudes weren't my fate
Purred louder than a lions roar
Eyes were larger than the moon
Meows let me know love was always new
followed me from room to room
even accepted my husband in '99
she never declined
somehow I knew
he was the one for sure
then she was my nurse
curled by me every day and night without jealously or remorse
as my belly grew each time with baby 1 and baby 2

never left my side
always wanted to stay inside
sleep in one spot
took care of our hearts
treated the babies like a nurse should
never scratched or bit although she could
how can I deny this feline
no need to lie
animals show emotions and love too
family is family no matter the species or two
then she started to wither
walking like a drunk
bones showing
doctors said tests showed nothing to fear
but it came one day
January 2007
Simba walked away
Never thought I could cry
A piece of me withered inside
That feline stayed by my side
continued and helped me till the day she died
couldn't hold back my tears
some never wanna hear
Simba was more than a cat to me
Simba taught me respect more
Simba taught me to care and love supplementary
She wanted to make sure I see
Love goes beyond what they told me
So I guess she left me when she was sure
My life was secure
Can't believe I can still weep
Simba was a cat to you but family to me
One day you may see and may even grieve

Over something so innocent and sweet with eyes of yellow,
blue or green
Fur soft and walking on fours
Making sure you know
Love and concern
Trust and loyalty
Care shouldn't have to hurt
Animals are just like us
Take notes and be aware
CARE...

ACKNOWLEDGEMENTS

the day in my home went by too fast
that moment in me will always last
your all welcomed at any time
for lemon drop martinis
oysters, fried fish
and of course some tea time...

Kira's Cup of Tea Inc.

Set design, Wardrobe, Styling!!!! ☺

Tanika Harris/DAVIS & COMPANY HAIR SALON

What u do with hair is such a stunning skill
Tanika your ability, proficiency and talent does more than pay
your bills.
The way you take time out
Your beauty shines inside and out
Proof of how God's love shines so bright,
Had to make you my honorary sister, cousin, friend till the end
with delight...

AD Lewis

Thank you AD for your makeup technique
I used to walk around bare
Make-up now is more fun than I thought
Not only used for a cover-up but as an art. I thank u...

Reuben Chandler/ Travis Lamont Lawson REDD LAW Creative Group

Your work
Is more than a work of art
Telling stories before they're even read
Thank you for your effects and panache...
Visions come to life; your eye makes sure,
Photos are your business and it shows how much you adore.
It was very nice that day you showed up at my door...

Mr. W. James Hunter/MJ IMAGES PHOTOGRAPHY & GRAPHIC DESIGN

Thank you for the beautiful book cover, layout and design style,
All your thoughts and knowledge you share far beyond compare
Photography is only one of your wonderful flairs
Teaching as you shoot is a gift shows you care
Seeing through the lens to the soul of your subjects
Forms your art into wondrous surprise
Fifty years strong and still blazing past your peers
A legend in your own years
Sharing crafts with all your peers
A friendship like yours is a friendship sincere...

William Pitts

Thank you so very much
The flashback photo was a beautiful surprise
Thanks for nice memories and positive vibes...